Behind the Mirror

Molly Maharaj Pinto

BookLeaf
Publishing

Presentation by *BookLeaf Publishing*

Web: www.bookleafpub.com

E-mail: info@bookleafpub.com

ISBN: 978-93-95755-49-8

First edition 2022

the unveiling

every day there's a curtain call and to your set
you must report
be it painful or be it unkind your scene is set
with you the star
how to make your role shine is up to you and
what you do
to make that scene one worthy of applause

a new day dawns and the stage is set with
sounds of welcome all around
fall not prey to lethargy or despair
each day brings little cues to guide you all day
through
lighting your path like beacons in the dark

be grateful for this ability that not everyone can
enjoy
another chance to try what slipped by before
put on that mask like an armour of strength
you are where you were meant to be as crazy as
that may be

it's only in embracing your role will you
recognition receive
so take the cue with every step and trust in the
Master's Plan

the joys the pains the laughter the tears
is a requisite for one to victorious be

a new day

at the end of every day
dusk covers you in its embrace
like the safety of the womb
be still for a while and you will know
the places you can't recall
and heal your tired bones

hush be still it's time for rest
dusk comes in without a pause
punctually at your door
there's no place for you to hide
no place you'd rather be
than in the quiet and still

as the earth goes spinning around
dusk returns without a sound
bringing respite from days of toil
even your body sighs and resigns
to the calling of man's biological call

good morning to a new sunrise
dusk now hides within her light
peeping through shadows cool
to let you know
it won't be long before repose

you got this

somebody asked me to speak of them
alas I can only put my thoughts in prose
but how does one summarise
the some total of another's life

my darling child I promise you this
there's been no mistake in who you are
as hard as it is for one to understand
when the soul cries out to injustice met

look back and you will see
every pain and every wound
was there to strengthen you
for all you face today

with time you will realise
every one's a pawn in this game of life
each playing his part without a clue
of why and how they do what they do

your task yes your task
is to look at life as a game of chess
studying each player as the pawn they are
and make your move as best for you

you are a masterpiece

don't waste your god given talents
it's not yours to keep
you're gonna have to account for it
or live in regret some day

you have so much to give
within the storehouse of your lives
each and every one logged
signed sealed and delivered

so take account of all you have
and use it as best you can
don't doubt the abilities that you have
they're more than you can count

wake up each day with determination
and claim them all you can
don't waste your time dreaming
of the way things used to be

yesterday has accumulated stuff
you willfully ignored
in chasing dreams that cannot exist
without hard work today

rainbows are for fairytales
hard labour is where you're at
your efforts will pave your way
to cross the oceans deep

I me myself

you are your own enemy
only you can harm yourself
no outside force can destroy you
except the body you wear

your journey is eternal
nothing learnt is ever lost
so fear not the outside
and hold fast on to your soul

the road is not a smooth one
with many a hairpin bend
you got to hold on tightly
to what is good within

be a unicorn

you can't change the world even if you try
but you can make a difference if you start with
yourself
concentrate on all you do and do it with total
concentration
offer your every action to the universe for that is
who you are
live each moment as an offering to the life you
have
it's sure to bring you happiness and success in
unexpected ways

don't discount a lucky catch or the early morning
alarm
it is in the very little things that blessings are to
be had
life is but an endless journey changing at every
sunrise
and you must cherish each morn and let go of
your past
whining or crying fretting or fuming won't take
you to where you must go
so smile you're on candid camera who knows
what surprise awaits you

the seasons come and go without your control
life is like the seasons your response is all you
own
to sunblock and enjoy a swim or snowboard
across the winter snow
this is the way of tribes of every nation and
culture across the globe
one tribe even survived a tsunami to the
wonderment of the scientific world
so is your survival make it a wonder for others
to know

I miss you mum

I miss my mum
and I know I always will
but there are things I do
which are reflections of you

as a mum today I've learnt
the horror of the pains you had
and I know it can't be undone
but here's a tribute of my love

mother you were self sacrificing
ever generous and mild
your wisdom was one of a kind
learnt from the battering of life

I will treasure that part of you in me
as my heart overflows with memories
of the love you poured on me
there'll be no other to replace you for me

lab rats

standing at a high point
watch the world go by
looks no different
than the rats within a lab

scurrying people everywhere
yet within their confines remain
tested with new viruses
outcomes garnered and defined

yes we're nothing less than lab rats
feeling mighty superior in our suites
watched under magnifying glass
the complexity of the human race

a new year

there's a silence unlike a holy night
this one born out of fear and not hope
many won't walk this journey with you
lost forever from this world they knew

and the curtain is slowly closing in
to another year filled with endless fears
many were lost in the battle of life
leaving a space that was theirs alone

but this world continues ceaselessly
gathering the dust as it goes
taking along the pain and hurt
moments of joy and laughter too

there will be no celebrations like the ones before
a silent war engulfs this world we know
a weapon of mass destruction like no other
before
has brought joyous revelry to a standstill once
more

yet with every sunrise new hope is assured
as human avatars continue doggedly

to seek find and obliterate
plagues and contagions that beset this world

so here's to a better tomorrow
freed from walls and masks
to get togethers and celebrations
and children playing everywhere

from a child to a man

today a child was born bringing joy and laughter
to his home
his life's plan tight within his fists he held
fearful of what it will unfold with each new
dawn
comforted and strengthened he grew strong
many hurdles he did climb bruising bumping as
he tarried on
doggedly determined to face the storms

today you stand a boy no more but still within
the child trembles
fearful of the mountain and sea enticingly
egging you on
bringing you joy and promising you hope
of a new dawn from the mountain tops
throw your dice and make your choice
you're born to win whatever the choice

when a child is born

watching a child grow is the hardest thing to do
with each new step they move farther from you
watching them stumble fumble and fall
the hardest thing to do is not reach out and catch
them
knowing full well the consequences of their
choice

the more stubborn a child the more pain for all
burning bridges leave smoke trails that chokes
and makes you cry
choosing gravel over a trodden lane is as foolish
as the ones before
bringing your child wisdom and you more pain
than when you walked the untrodden paths now
worn bare

the gurgles and smiles the hugs and kisses
has no inkling of the hurdles ahead
maternal calling another trick of the universe
to procreate for the continuation of this
experimentation
a trap you can't escape programmed to continue
this crazy charade
be wise be strong that choice is yours

envy beware

why do you envy the one who gains fame
nobody's stopping you from walking in his shoes
the man on the top never stopped for beers and
skittles
nor bothered with pleasures or endless musings
so tell me why do you hate their success so

the one who advanced ahead of you in life
grabbed his life with both his hands molding it
into the life he planned
taking nothing for granted chance or fate
crafted a life out of sacrifice and pain
so tell me again why do you envy this person
you see

I do believe the envy sees failure highlighted in
achievers
while the wise find ways to be the success they
see
be not envious of the ones who triumph
their tailored suits hide the scars of life
the price paid is not for the weak so why do you
envy him so

protagonist

beware of the evil that lurks within you
his fangs are vicious and will totally destroy you
he is hungry and deceitful as wily as can be
changing your heart to stone and making it mean

beware of the quiet voice that whispers to you
glorifying your successes and rendering you
vain
poisoning your system till all you ever feel
is envy and insecurity fear without cause

beware I tell you of that serpent wrapped around
your spine
never feed it or it will grow and render you blind
turning your thinking from goodness to sin
repeating history and playing you for a pawn

pride goes before a fall

wise words were said from a soul that broke
under the stronghold of the yoke of pride
foolish men who in pomposity revel
beware the wrath this world won't spare

be humble in everything you do
in honesty your peace and prosperity find
pride endorses lies and lies endorses pain
when alone with your conscience you must
remain

when a man fears nothing and sleeps a sound
sleep
wearing his truth like an armour it's hard to
penetrate
truly this man knows happiness like few can
ever dream
for with him there is nothing for you to trade

ego walks in stilettos

careful be thy steps or wise ones
precarious is your journey
just a slip and you will find
earth between your teeth

wicked ego cunning and so quiet
even at birth your tentacles start
carefully snaring your victims at will
with each victory your power expanding

each passing day you polish your skills
encouraged and aided by endless cajolery
stealthily devouring the very hands that feed
playing your victim at your will

you're the leader and you're the killer
difference be small whatever your style
conquering and trampling in your stilettos high
your humbling force is from on high

who is a mother

a mother is a nurturer of four legged or two
she need not carry this being within her classic
womb
she's born out of love and compassion
she's a mother who nurtures wherever the need
calls

there are mothers and there are mothers
it's a term not one fits all
she that loves and gives her everything
her sleep her comfort her time health and all

I know a woman who does this for animals big and
small
who's given up her happiness in search for her
furry kids
she's a mother to remember when this day you
recall
a mother born out of sacrifice and compassion is a
mother I recall

let's give a toast to mothers whether living or gone
the ones who bore this duty to the forlorn
remember every mother whatever may be her
calling
a mother is sacrifice heartache and pain

odyssey of life

it's hard keeping up with the business of this
world
it weighs heavy on all with its worries and its
cares
oh to be free to walk the mountains and sail the
seas
never to fear or worry of what tomorrow might
be

I'm ever grateful to my parents for giving up
their dreams
to be my parent and help me find myself
they lost every penny in the pursuit of my
ambitions
and died unfulfilled at the end of their lives

what would I be if my parents never cared
if like an animal I was left to go my own way
I'd probably be dead or starving in the cold
the sacrifice of my parents ensured the passage
of my life

oh how much you suffered in parenting me
even in death you share my every joy and every
pain

will your suffering ever find refuge and peace
or would this eternal suffering be the journey of
our lives

happiness is a shooting star

fleetingly bright and dead in a flash
a happy face is not a happy soul
just a giftwrap over all life's pains
may your spark stay ever bright even in the
darkest times

the fashion queen dreams to be free
from the lights and endless fasting
the prize of luxury takes a heavy toll
don't be fooled by their haughty walk

what is this freedom that you seek
look within there lies your keys
even the birds you often wish to be
must live in fear of endless perils

but you my friend have a chance to be
happy and free if you please
just finding joy in little things
tomorrow is yet a distant dream

life is but an eternal wheel
reaping and sowing and sowing again
a bountiful harvest will in persistence be
love is the seed wherever you may be

a toast to women

women of grace don't fall to disgrace
shouting and screaming won't win you a place
you're mighty and strong and can take on the
world
but spare me downsizing to what you're above

you know where you come from and what you
can wield
so quit fighting for equal rights fight for freedom
I say
rise to the occasion of being who you are
a woman of courage beauty and grace

no male could ever be standing today
be it human animal insect or plant
none could survive without the female to thrive
I tell you right now that even the powers on high
needed a woman to survive

you're more powerful than you were allowed to
believe
you have the power in your very grace
arise every woman of every size shape or form
you are the power but you just don't know